Alistai
story oj
the natiυιι υj Scotland.

The observations are astute, the parallel is stark and the prophetic call is clear: 'Scotland, come to your senses!'

Peter Anderson
City on a Hill, Edinburgh

Acknowledgements

First, thank You, Father, for allowing me back into Your house.

Second, I am grateful to you, my kind family and friends, who took the time to offer really valuable feedback on my draft and encouraged me to put this into print.

Third, I grudgingly acknowledge Covid – without its enforced confinement, this would never have seen the light of day!

Alistair

July 2022

Introduction

The most wonderful moment in the Prodigal Son's life comes at his lowest point.

Jesus describes that moment in a simple yet profound way ... '... *He came to his senses.*'

By running from God, we also flee our senses ... but then, when we return to our senses, we 'come home' to a loving Father.

Living in 21st century Scotland, I reflect on how my nation, over 250 years, has run off and squandered an astonishing spiritual legacy ... but like many, I also dream of a widespread return to sense.

After all, as this little booklet ends with my own personal testimony, if it can happen for me, then why not for us?

But first, the story ...

The Prodigal Son

Jesus continued: 'There was a man who had two sons. The younger one said to his father, "Father, give me my share of the estate." So he divided his property between them.

'Not long after that, the younger son got together all he had, set off for a distant country and there squandered his wealth in wild living. After he had spent everything, there was a severe famine in that whole country, and he began to be in need. So he went and hired himself out to a citizen of that country, who sent him to his fields to feed pigs. He longed to fill his stomach with the pods that the pigs were eating, but no one gave him anything.

'When he came to his senses, he said, "How many of my father's hired servants have food to spare, and here I am starving to death! I will set out and go back to my father and say to him: Father, I have sinned against heaven and against you. I am no longer worthy to be called your son; make me like one of your hired servants." So he got up and went to his father.

'But while he was still a long way off, his father saw him and was filled with compassion for him; he ran to his son, threw his arms round him and kissed him.

'The son said to him, "Father, I have sinned against heaven and against you. I am no longer worthy to be called your son."

'But the father said to his servants, "Quick! Bring the best robe and put it on him. Put a ring on his finger and sandals on his feet. Bring the fattened calf and kill it. Let's have a feast and celebrate. For this son of mine was dead and is alive again; he was lost and is found." So they began to celebrate.

(Luke 15:11-24; New International Version)

When He Came to His Senses

"When he came to his senses, he said, 'How many of my father's hired servants have food to spare, and here I am starving to death! I will set out and go back to my father and say to him: Father, I have sinned against heaven and against you. I am no longer worthy to be called your son; make me like one of your hired servants.'

The Prodigal Son, LUKE 15:17-20 (NIV)

The Prodigal Son's life bottomed out in a very low place.

In Jesus' timeless parable, when the squandering and debauchery were finally over, the young man, at the very end of himself, finally *"came to his senses."* In repentance, his stubborn dam of wilful resistance to the blindingly obvious finally crumbled.

Decide for yourself whether tears flowed — it's certainly hard to properly enter the drama and leave with a dry eye.

Perhaps the greatest emotion is simply one of relief — relief that he has, at long last, woken up from the interminable binge that descended from self-deception to self-gratification to self-destruction.

Mentally and spiritually, he must have been very sore headed. But at least he was now sober.

His inheritance is spent. Nothing in his pocket. Zilch.

His delusions have stripped him bare. Nothing left to lose, no one to struggle with, nothing to strive for.

Bankrupt but alive ... or maybe just a dead man walking.

With nothing left to his name and no father to appeal to, his earlier sense of entitlement was long gone. His poverty was more than simply material as he looked up to the pigs, bereft of any self-value.

His belly may be empty, but at least he is now, at long last, in his right mind, ready to clean up and try anything he can think of to find some means of survival.

He decides to about-turn and set off home again. That's all he knows, the only place his senses are able to lead him. It's not just his best shot; it's his only shot.

But whether he realises it or not, from this day forward, from this place of nothingness, he has found an asset that, though it didn't come with his share in his father's estate, will go with him for the rest of his life. A priceless asset.

That asset is knowledge.

Sense.

As Jesus put it, *"… He came to his senses."*

These senses would include, most valuably, intimate knowledge of his Number 1 enemy in life.

Himself.

And so, ironically, this shattering of his youthful, testosterone-driven ambition, this breaking of his pride, this place of humiliation, promised to be his making as a man.

Death – the best word for it – doesn't come easy, but that, as Jesus taught, is the only place to find life. His moment of awakening may have taken some time coming, but surely it would now never leave him. He could never un-see what he had seen or un-know what was now known.

From here on in, in all his future dealings and relationships, the pig's trough will be an elephant in the room, a silent presence in his conversations, adding context to his thinking, tampering with his attitudes, cautioning his speech, questioning his motives. It will forbid him ever to grumble about his father. It will turn into a full body mirror should he ever find fault with his older brother. His testimony of personal failure, repentance and forgiveness will eyeball him when he hardens, tap him on the chest when he gets proud, block the door when he tries to walk out the room.

Jesus tells us it was looking enviously at the pigs that finally brought this Jewish prodigal to his senses. That's what it took. That's how low he had to sink.

Coming to his senses, however, was about so much more than head knowledge and making right mental assessments. It was a deeply spiritual thing, a place of personal epiphany that would radically impact and transform his entire life. It was basically a change of heart. The heated passions of youth would now, through his brokenness, be replaced by a contrite heart and a humble spirit.

He now had painful yet priceless hind sights that would convert into lifelong moral indebtedness ... *'What a fool I've been! How could I not have seen what I was doing? Why did I not listen? What untold damage and hurt did I cause? It's so, so obvious now ... Oh God, forgive me for what I've been and done to You, and to those who loved me.'*

Coming to his senses would mean being rooted and grounded in a place of humility!

It would be more than just a case of, *'There, but for the grace of God, **go** I!'* ... For him it was, *'There – despite the grace of God – **went** I!'*

Heart and mind always go hand in hand, talking to each other, feeding off and influencing each other. It works negatively as well as positively. Human beings have always been good at spin, crafting moral narratives to justify the inexcusable, to get us off the hook, to disarm opponents to our ambitions, and, perhaps most importantly, to relieve inner discomfort about doing what we're going to do anyway. If we can't convince ourselves, how can we convince anyone else?

All this may seem a negative view of human nature, but it's a biblical observation that's been played out countless times throughout human history. The prophet Jeremiah (17:9) said *"the heart is deceitful above all things,"* and we shouldn't be amazed at what the heart is able to talk the mind into coming up with, to justify what we want to do!

It's amazing how the heart and mind can collaborate to make nonsense sound reasonable! There's no end to what we can be bought into believing. We have to talk ourselves into it too. We need to create a sense of feel-good or wellbeing about doing things that are ... well ... bad.

And we have to work hard at it because there is something inside even the darkest heart that, though marred by sin, was placed there by God when he created mankind in His own image: a moral conscience, gifted by common grace to every human being alive.

It's that part of us that, no matter how far we run, no matter how much we try to anaesthetise our senses with substances, pleasures and pursuits, keeps prodding us from the inside, saying, *That's wrong.*

We may try to alleviate our discomfort with moral painkillers ... *But no one's perfect ... You did what you had to do ... They deserved it ... It was the lesser of two evils ... Anyone would have done the same ...* – and one of the most popular of all, yet spoken with almost moralistic force – *You mustn't feel guilty ...*

Welcome to the mushy morality of the modern West!

Pardon me, but if I *am* guilty, shouldn't I *feel* guilty? Is it not natural and right to feel like what you are?

Guilt is a moral pain sensor through which the soul speaks.

Sure, guilt is too frequently projected in an unhealthy manner. Satan is described in the Bible as *"the accuser of the brethren"* (Rev. 12:10) and we know how the scribes and Pharisees, Jesus' No. 1 enemies, literally peddled guilt for a living. Guilt can be, and often is, used as a weapon of evil intent. Absolutely.

But still, more fundamentally, the ability to feel guilt is a moral gift from God.

Like a rash on the body or a high temperature, a sense of guilt will come when we've sinned. Guilt is an indicator of something not being right. And the antidote to sin is not denial, but repentance.

The one-liner 'moral painkillers' I alluded to above, like any painkiller, only treat the symptoms, not the cause, offering temporary comfort without dealing with the condition. They may contain elements of truth and tide us over until we get the proper treatment, but they don't get to the root of the problem, make us healthy, or transform us for the better.

Numbing the symptoms may alleviate discomfort for the moment, but what we really need is for the underlying problem, the cause of the guilt, either to be dealt with or to pass.

Symptoms are our body speaking to us, sometimes screaming at us, that something is not right. It's not enough to shut them up. We need to listen to what they're saying. They may be telling us to go to a doctor for diagnosis. The last thing we want to do is ignore emergency signals at the preventative stages of something that may be serious.

When a woman was caught committing adultery and paraded before Jesus by the Pharisees for condemnation, He didn't say to her, *'Don't listen to these bad people* (even though that was what they were) ... *Your sexual lifestyle is no business of theirs. I've come to affirm your moral value! You've only sinned if you're lying to yourself! ...'*

No – that moral universe doesn't belong to Jesus!

He didn't need to condemn her (although He did frequently condemn the Pharisees!), because she, He, they and everyone else already knew she was guilty.

Doctor Jesus' approach to this morally sick woman began, not by saying she wasn't a sinner, but by pointing out that all her accusers were too. He went on to deal with the problem by relieving her pain with forgiveness – *"Neither do I condemn you …"* – and ended by sending her off with a prescription to prevent recurrence: *"Go your way and sin no more!"* (John 8:11)

This woman came to Jesus sinful. End of. But she left Him forgiven, cleansed of guilt, pure as a virgin, empowered for a fresh start, and loved by a merciful God.

Nowhere in the Gospels does Jesus say to anyone, *'You shouldn't feel bad about sin!'*

This is why, when I imagine the Prodigal, sitting with the pigs, rehearsing his words, *"Father, I have sinned against heaven and against you. I am no longer worthy to be called your son …"* I imagine a tear-bathed face.

He was cut to the heart, in remorse over what he had done because of what he had become. His personal failure left him disconsolate and broken, ashamed and pleading from within for mercy that he knew he didn't deserve. This is what heart repentance is, and it's the only place where sense is truly found.

It happened to me when I was a young man of 18, and I'd like to share about the night I too came to my senses, but I also care deeply about my nation, modern Scotland, and in recent years I've come to see my people personified in the Prodigal Son.

Like the Prodigal of Luke chapter 15, we inherited so, so much and had everything to lose, and yet now we seem to have blown it all away. It didn't happen overnight, though, and the seeds of our wayward heart were being sown even in the halcyon days of Scotland's 16th century Reformation and 18th century Enlightenment.

As with the Prodigal Son, even before we 'left home' as a people, a wayward heart was already twisting our thinking, chipping away at our senses, undermining once unquestioned beliefs and values, preparing us for a future where anything would go, where we would one day waken up in a pigsty.

A Prodigal Nation

"Righteousness exalts a nation, but sin is a disgrace to any people."

PROVERBS 14:34

Implicit in Jesus' description of the Prodigal's turn-around as *'coming to his senses'* is the understanding that when he departed from God, he fled his senses.

This seems to be pretty much what has happened to Scotland over the past two centuries.

Oh, some good, even great, things have happened, and occasionally still happen. There can be wonderful, heroic moments of valour in a sinking ship. But the general direction has been downwards.

I think few Scots today are remotely aware of the dizzying heights our little nation was once elevated to – and even less know what it was that raised us to these heights. If we were more aware of these faded glories, in both church and national life, we'd be more than shocked by where we are today.

The Scriptures declare that *"righteousness exalts a nation,"* (Proverbs 14:34) and when God's in charge everything seems to go well, almost to the point where it can be taken for granted. Conversely, when a people turn away from Him, everything else starts to go awry.

Like the Prodigal starting off happy, living off Dad's inheritance money, God-inspired institutions can run along for a while on reserves accrued, not to mention the reputation earned by founding pioneers who walked with God. They get so used to enjoying what's been bequeathed that they can deceive themselves into thinking they did it themselves and start to wing it on their own.

But before long we're selling off the capital to pay the workers, and things start to dry up. Our forefathers got what they got because they walked with God. And they only got what they got because, ultimately, what they wanted was God.

But if people turn away from God, it's not just Him they lose; eventually they lose what He gave them too.

It happened in ancient Judah half a millennium before Jesus.

The Jews departed from God well before they were deported into foreign captivity. The journey from evil intent to the pig pen is no overnight expedition. Its biggest falls can take a very long time, and the descent can seem almost imperceptible as the glory fades.

It took centuries for the ancient Jewish people to fall from the heights of David's Zion to the depths of Nebuchadnezzar's Babylon, but the first seeds were sown in the glory days of David himself, when the king summoned his neighbour's wife into his bed chamber. Before we know it, his sons are breaking his heart, his descendants are going to war, the kingdom's being torn in two, and, eventually, after numerous derided warnings by God's prophets, Jerusalem – temple, palace, city, the lot – is looted and destroyed, and a people who once feared God are dragged off into captivity by the most fearful dictator of the day.

With hindsight, every downfall is inevitable. But at the time, it's by degrees and can be so subtle. One of the most striking marks of the greatest falls is the amount of sheer denial that accompanies the downward trajectory.

Nations rise and nations fall.

It's relatively easy for a Scot, from thousands of miles away, to see history playing itself out again today in America, the most modern nation to have been so wonderfully blessed by God. Yet now, they appear to be becoming more like us in Europe, starting to become ashamed of, and estranged from, God. Yes, some great things do still happen there, and there'll be a few more yet, but we can see the general trajectory on the graph. Looking west towards their sunset, things do seem to be accelerating. Their red orb is falling to that point, just above the horizon, where it starts to go down very fast … *'Quickly, get the camera out before we lose it!'*

Before America, it was the British Empire, with little Scotland very much at the helm. To quote the most prominent Scottish historian of our time, Sir Tom Devine, *"At the height of the British Empire, England may have ruled the world, but Scots ran it."* Professor Devine suggests that no other small country has more disproportionately engaged with and influenced the modern world. And when Johns Hopkins University history professor, Arthur Herman, an American without a drop of Scottish blood, entitled his 2002 best seller, *"How the Scots Invented the Modern World"*, no serious academic attempted to deny the substance of his work, focusing on the 18th century Enlightenment period forward.

But the Scottish Enlightenment didn't arrive out of nowhere. As much as any nation has been known to, Scotland had honoured God and embraced the Scriptures in the post-Reformation 16th and 17th centuries. It was a tiny Bible loving country of never more than a couple of million souls that found itself raised to spectacular levels of global influence in the 18th and 19th centuries.

The 1500s began with perhaps one of our most unsung spiritual heroes, Patrick Hamilton, a beautiful man of God. The recently married 24-year-old was already an eminent spiritual leader and academic when he was burnt at the stake in St Andrews on the 15th of February 1528. Like the first Christian martyr, Stephen, he refused to retaliate and prayed for his murderers as they took hours over his half-botched execution. The stone slab marked *'PH'* can still be found in St Andrews today.

Of noble background, Hamilton had cross-pollinated with some of the great European reformers of the early 16th century before returning to scatter precious Gospel seed up and down his beloved homeland. He preached a simple message of repentance and faith in Jesus Christ, free of all the dead ritual, superstition, and ceremony of power-corrupted religion. He distributed pamphlets and preached the Good News wherever and to whomever he could, all the time inspiring those who would follow in his steps, men like George Wishart, John Knox and so many more.

It was Tertullian who famously wrote, *"The blood of the martyrs is the seed of the church"*, and I for one would have no problem with a certain Patrick (not the one of Irish yore), rather than Andrew, being the patron saint of Scotland, because it was the faith, courage and sacrifice of men like Hamilton that released centuries of untold blessing from God upon our tiny nation.

God didn't just arbitrarily parachute the blessing down from heaven; He birthed it through the vision of apostolic leaders, men gifted, trained, and raised up for their time. Our nation's spiritual endowment may have been unprecedented, but it was no accident. In fact, when we see *how* it unfolded, there almost seems an inevitability about it.

The vision and strategy of Scotland's 16th century reformers, John Knox the most famous, which became a national driver for the next three centuries, was reduced to five words:

A school for every parish!

Scotland's 17th century Education Acts went on to legislate that every community should have its own highly and broadly educated school master, conducting a church-led and supervised plan of universal education. The goal was to produce a fully literate population, with the explicit purpose that the Scriptures be placed in the hands, and planted in the hearts, of every boy and girl in the land.

The result of this vision was that, by the mid-18th century, Lowland Scotland was to have the most literate and educated populace ever known. From now on, education was no longer to be for the elite, but for the masses. Scotland itself, by the mid-1700s, was too small to contain this revolution of learning, as emigrants poured out into the New World with literacy rates of 75% and more, rising to prominence wherever they went and disproportionately shaping the modern world. The momentum continued all the way through the 19th century, Scotland still even outpacing England, where primary education wasn't made compulsory until 1889, 17 years later than in Scotland.

It's a huge amount of history and a lot of years to reduce to so few words, but the most widely celebrated eventual outcome of the reformers' vision was what would be globally marvelled at as the 18th century Scottish Enlightenment. It was an explosion of genius that, in its day, caused renowned academics like French philosopher Voltaire and his peers simply to look on in awe. English nobility abandoned the stagnant waters of their only two universities, Oxford and Cambridge, to send their children to one of Scotland's five, as all of Europe looked to Edinburgh, Glasgow, Aberdeen (two universities at the time) and St Andrews, for what Voltaire saw in our forefathers as *"the highest ideals of civilisation."*

But it wasn't learning for learning's sake that produced the educated population that the Scottish Enlightenment emerged out of and so capitalised upon; it was education for the Gospel's sake.

'A school for every parish' had been the trumpeted vision of Scotland's evangelical Reformers nearly two centuries before the Scottish Enlightenment. Their vision became the means by which not just the Scottish nation, but the entire modern world was, both directly and indirectly, so powerfully impacted by our forefathers' evangelical Christian faith.

But to appreciate the Scotland moment, we need to go another couple of centuries further back again.

In the late 1300s, the man dubbed the 'morning star' of the Reformation, Oxford professor John Wycliffe, saw, spoke and did pretty much everything that Martin Luther was to become so famous for more than a century after him, and most notably translated the Scriptures out of Latin into the vernacular of the common man. But his work made no immediately transforming impact on his own nation, let alone Europe. Why? One significant reason was his inability to widely disseminate what he had translated.

What use was it to translate the Scriptures, if there is no means of publishing what's been translated?

A major reason (although there are obviously others) why it was Luther, rather than Wycliffe, who heralded the actual sunrise of the Reformation, with Wycliffe merely the pre-dawn 'morning star', was because of something that happened mid-way in between the two of them.

In 1452, in the German town of Mainz, Johannes Guttenberg launched the world's first printing press, with the express purpose of publishing the Bible in the common vernacular. Three years later, the first 180 copies of the Guttenberg Bible were produced. The printed page, which would grow into what we have come to know as the mass media, was birthed for such a moment.

But there was another, much bigger problem yet.

What use is it to publish the Scriptures in the language of the people, if the people are illiterate?

Enter Scotland's moment!

The explosive, world-changing influence of post-Reformation Scotland, culminating in the 18th century's twin-pronged Scottish Enlightenment and Industrial Revolution, was no accident.

It was not Knox's supposed prayer – *'Give me Scotland 'ere I die!'* – that made him such an apostle of change in both church and nation, but his 'big picture' vision: *A school for every parish!*

Yes, Scotland's schools were to be a place of broad learning, but the dynamic that justified, generated, and guided them was to be the

Gospel of Jesus Christ, and the ability of every child in the land to independently read and apprehend the Scriptures. Parish schools, overseen by an evangelical church, were not just to be places of literacy and numeracy for useful citizens; they were to be a modern-day 'hall of Tyrannus' in every community, where disciples would be raised in the knowledge and service of Jesus Christ.

Without this Gospel vision, Scotland could never possibly have been lifted from the most under-developed backwater of pre-Reformation Europe to the world-leading heights of the late-18th and 19th centuries. It was this period, when Edinburgh would emerge as the 'Athens' of the European Enlightenment and Glasgow as the 'engine room' of the British Empire, that moved Herman to write his remarkable tribute to Scotland's heyday. These heady times would simply never have arrived, had Knox's vision not produced the most literate and numerate population on earth within two centuries of his death.

So how disappointing it is that some of those who had benefitted most from the lavish inheritance of a church-bequeathed education system, should, like the Prodigal Son, turn from God and 'make off' with their share of the inheritance. Such prodigals, far from a new phenomenon in Scotland, were led by the likes of the much-vaunted doyen of Enlightenment philosophy, Edinburgh atheist David Hume who, while living off Knox's legacy, preferred to sow the seeds of scepticism for generations to come.

Though now elevated to the top of the Scottish intellectual firmament (with Knox long since demoted to historical punchbag), Hume, though highly respected, was far from uniquely revered among his Scottish contemporaries. His Kirkcaldy peer, Adam Smith, was a more influential thinker in his time, both at home and in the New World, as were two Christian ministers who sat in the chairs of moral philosophy in Aberdeen's and Glasgow's universities, Thomas Reid and Frances Hutcheson.

Unlike their Edinburgh colleague, Reid and Hutcheson were Christians who believed that when we depart from God, we also begin to lose a grip of our senses. Maybe Reid had this in mind as he founded what came to be known as the *Common Sense* school of philosophy. (Yes, that *is* where the term 'common sense' came from!) But just as ancient Judah's eventual fall from glory began at the height of David's empire, so the seeds of our nation's departure from its spiritual senses were already being sown at the apex of Scotland's Enlightenment.

For example, Hume subscribed to the 'Ideal' school of philosophy espoused by Locke, Descartes before him and numerous ancient Greeks too. One of the luxurious ideas these professional thinkers indulged in was the theory that, as humans, we do not actually have any direct knowledge of the external world; all we have is a subjective awareness that interprets and transmits to us what our sense organs tell us. But beyond our own fallible awareness, we can never be certain whether what we think we see is real or not. Ultimately, we have no absolute guarantee that anything we're sure exists, actually exists.

Most sensible people are at this point thinking, *My goodness!*

I'm thinking, *Thank goodness for Thomas Reid!*

Reid summed up philosophical indulgences such as the 'Ideal' theory, ideas that take no one anywhere useful, in one word: Nonsense! Reid dismissed the Ideal theory, asking how millions of people, simultaneously observing the same world, could possibly be experiencing the exact same illusion, without even a whisper between them. It was 'common sense'.

Reid's common sense was based on the simple belief that God has imbued every human being, regardless of where they are or when they live, with the innate ability to make the same deductions, not just about what they observe in the natural world, but about things that are right and wrong. Reid echoed the observation of Paul, in

Romans chapters 1 and 2, where he teaches that even those who have never known the laws of Scripture have no excuse for doing wrong, because God has created them all to know from within themselves.

And yet, it's a frightening phenomenon that societies, just like individuals, can, as the Prodigal did, wilfully turn from their senses, virtually *en masse*. It's frightening because nonsense isn't harmless.

By the time the Prodigal Son finally left home, senseless thinking and a poisoned heart were already feeding off each other to fuel what would end up a debauched and dangerous lifestyle. Cast adrift from previously unquestioned certainties, he would soon find himself bobbing about aimlessly on an endless ocean, where nothing is certain and anything is possible, nowhere out of bounds, little to be trusted, everything to be questioned. All the Prodigal can now do is judge what seems best for him and, if it brings pleasure, call it good for today; if it doesn't, call it bad for now. But everything might change tomorrow, in a God-less, anchor-less world where there are no absolutes or certainties anymore.

When we turn from God and even deny His existence, it's not a big leap, as Hume and others demonstrated, to question whether anything really exists or matters any more. When we reject the Creator, creation has nothing to stand on.

Hutcheson and Reid maybe foresaw where Hume and others would lead our nation, as they and their contemporaries increasingly looked across the Atlantic towards another dawn, among a more faith-dependant migrant people, from which they expected much. The early pioneers of that emerging nation looked back eagerly to them also, as they prepared the architectural drawings of their new super-nation. These Founding Fathers didn't have the luxury of building their country's future on anything as flimsy as *you-can-never-know-for-certain*. It was life or death for them, the stakes were too high, and their dreams of a great future required faith and biblical hope. They couldn't afford to bank their destiny on the scepticism of Hume, so they fed on the Christian certainties of Hutcheson and Reid, while declaring, *'In God we trust!'*

"We hold these truths to be self-evident, that all men are created equal ...", enshrined in the US Declaration of Independence, is drawn directly from Thomas Reid's Common Sense school of philosophy, where reliable truth is always just that: *self-evident*. It's common sense. John Adams and Thomas Jefferson, the second and third US Presidents, were deeply influenced, not just by Reid but by his protégé Dugald Stewart, not to mention their friends Frances Hutcheson, John Witherspoon (a US Founding Father himself) and many other Scots, as they sought to lay the bedrock for 'one nation under God.'

As America, like Scotland and ancient Judah in times past, sets off from the faith of its Founding Fathers, the questions are the same as they were for the Prodigal Son: How far will they drift? How low will they sink? Will they ever come home?

We know how low the Prodigal sank. But at least he did bottom out. The modern Western world is still in spiritual and moral freefall.

How senseless can our nation become, this little land that once birthed the School of Common Sense?

I think many readers will know the kinds of things I'm thinking about. We live in a land where, from the ruins of a once-towering national church to the post-Christian culture of our public institutions, few are bold enough to be certain about anything anymore.

It appears to be no longer obvious, for example, that Christian marriage is a lifelong, monogamous, heterosexual relationship; nor even a simple observation that men and women are male and female adult human beings. Such basic truths are no longer self-evident.

Troublingly, it's more than a pitiful state of confusion; there's something highly dogmatic, even compulsive, coming out of today's mountain of academia. A learned elite, the high priesthood of so called 'progressive' ideology, now forbids us and our children to be certain about once unquestioned truths.

As we hurtle downwards, we are even taught to be ashamed of beliefs and values embraced on the way up. Of course, we surely got some things wrong on the upward journey – there never was a perfect age – but something precious has been lost. Something has died.

We are far from home.

If ever a people needed to come to its senses, it is now.

But I can't look down condescendingly upon a prodigal people without seeing myself among them. Like the Prodigal Son, my own past is an invisible reminder that I should only, ever feel grateful, never superior. I cannot say, *'There, but for the grace of God, go I;'* rather, *'There, despite the grace of God, went I!'*

I suppose we all at times despair at the state of the world around us. But these are the times when we can so easily forget some of the places we've been ourselves; like the mornings we rush out without checking the mirror and vent our frustrations on a universe that just isn't getting it right!

Of course, when our heart attitude is right, we will be deeply concerned about a prodigal world, and that concern is appropriate in people who truly care. But it must also be tempered by the fact that the change I long to see must always begin with me.

We need to weep for a prodigal nation rather than scream at it, and *leading* people back to their senses is always more effective than *pointing* them back. This is something I find so endearing about Scottish people, especially in Glasgow. When you ask them directions in the street, their response will often be, *'Och, just come wi' me – I'm going that way myself!'*

I think that's the kind of church that God could best use to bring Scotland back to its senses, in any age, never mind the modern one. Qualities of humility and self-scrutiny may even have been lacking in our nation 'on the way up', but who am I to say?

I can think of no better way to conclude these thoughts on a prodigal nation than to quote one of my distant heroes, Dallas pastor Tony Evans …

> *"If you want a better world, composed of better nations, inhabited by better states, filled with better counties, made up of better cities, comprised of better neighbourhoods, illuminated by better churches, populated by better families, then you'll have to start by becoming a better person … It all starts with you!"*

If There's Hope for Me

Amazing Grace, how sweet the sound
That saved a wretch like me
I once was lost, but now am found
Was blind but now I see

It all started with me at around 4 o'clock in the morning on Saturday, 6th February 1982 in Room B221 of Glasgow's Wolfson Hall of Residence. That's when I first came to my senses.

On that dark night, even though still only eighteen years of age, I realised in my heart, and my mind couldn't argue, that this was probably my last chance. If my life didn't turn around now, it was all over. I say *last* chance because God had given me another one a year previously, before I left home, when I had the most frightening experience.

From nowhere, my mind was invaded by horrible, evil thoughts over which I had no control. Thankfully, because of what happened next, I no longer remember those thoughts today. In panic and fear, I walked into my parents' bedroom where I knew I would find a Bible, the only thing I could think of to turn to.

Sitting down on the bed, I picked up the Bible and, holding it in my hand, I opened it, not knowing where to read. I still don't recall what I read, but I have never forgotten what happened within me. As suddenly as the mental storm had arisen, it subsided, the thoughts disappeared, and a calm peace settled over me.

Then a new struggle began, an inner tug of war. What was I to do with this? Was I to become a Christian now? I could see an open invitation before me. I could have walked right through, there and then, and become a born-again believer. It was real.

But I wavered at the fence.

What would my friends think? It would be a real shock. In the circles I'd made home, I'd be an instant laughingstock. My friends would be gone, to be replaced by nothing. The things I enjoyed, the drunkenness and parties, would have to stop. Even the cigarettes would have to go. The language would have to clean up too. School, totally on my own, would be awful.

No, it was all just too much to give up.

Still, I knew at that moment, more than ever before, that God was real, and that it was possible, even attractive, to know and walk with Him in life.

Maybe some other day … but now?

I 'took the goods' and left the room extremely relieved.

But as I turned my back on my Benefactor, I knew two things: first, I owed God one; and second, if I didn't say yes to such an offer should it come a second time, the chances are that I never would.

I hadn't left home yet but, in my heart, it wasn't long before I'd be heading off to the wide-open spaces of the big city, with nothing to restrain me and no one to worry (so I thought) about the riotous and chaotic binge my life would descend into.

How I even made it to university was quite a feat as, throughout my school years, I barely opened a book, rarely doing homework let alone studying for exams. I recall, as a 15-year-old out on the streets with my pals the night before my O-Grade Latin (- my friends were bemused by that one), ducking up a side-street as my teacher walked past.

But then, early in my final year of secondary school, the headmaster called me into his office, not on this occasion to inform me that he was sending another letter home on account of my persistent lateness, lack of school uniform or smoking behind the bike sheds, but to inquire as to what I intended to do with my life. Seeing it as my ticket off the Isle of Lewis, I informed him I was thinking of going to university to study psychology or something like that.

He nearly choked.

"I don't think so," he began, *"not the way you're going. You may have sailed through your O-Grades without working, but Highers are a different matter. Unless there's a serious change, I think you need to think of something else."*

Hmmm, *"I don't think so …"*, says he!

It was the moment he said that that, for the first time in my life, I decided to study. That winter, out of sheer defiance and desperation to leave home, I virtually chain-smoked my way through Vergil's Aeneid, Kelvin's Law and French subjunctives, to leave behind me both school and stunned friends, as I set off for the University of Glasgow with six Highers.

I'll never forget the moment I arrived in the room I would soon turn into my own personal 'pigsty'. It was well into September and, looking out onto the green fields to the rear, my eyes suddenly bulged as I spotted a sizeable harvest of thin, long-stemmed psilocybin, commonly known as 'magic mushrooms'. Immediately, I pulled out a polythene bag, abandoned my unopened luggage and made for the door. Barely arrived and I was already gone.

I'd been introduced to this psychedelic fungus by a teenage friend called Derek. Though an intelligent guy, Derek had left school at just 16 and travelled to Poona in India to join the ashram of Sannyasin cult leader Bhagwan Shree Rajneesh. He returned to Scotland a year later, dressed in bright orange, wearing beads with Bhagwan's long-bearded face in their locket, announcing his new name personally given by Bhagwan, 'Swami Anand Nirmal', sharing his guru's literature, introducing lost souls like me to Dynamic Meditation … and showing where best to look for psilocybin mushrooms (– I've never since been surprised to meet hippies 'partial to a round of golf'!).

It's amazing how far a prodigal will go. How did I get to there from ...?

My dad was a gracious Christian man. (My mother was a great spiritual influence too, but I'll stick to the Prodigal Son narrative here.) Some fifty years older than I, Dad passed away just six days short of his 94th birthday, in 2007. I do not recall one day in more than forty years that he didn't begin and end by reading his Bible and praying. He was a merchant navy captain, often away at sea, but whenever he was at home, in my early childhood, every night he gathered the family – my mother, older brother and sister, and me – around him for family worship, as we read from the Psalms and New Testament before all kneeling over our chairs while he led us in prayer. This may seem ritualistic, but it was also deeply foundational. It was the 'father's house' that this prodigal would one day run from.

I remember one sunny summer Sunday afternoon on holiday, my dad helping me, barely 9 years old, to memorise the marathon answer to the 18th Question of the Shorter Catechism of the Westminster Confession of Faith – I could easily recite it here and now, half a century later, but I fear I'd lose the ones I most want to be reading this! Although clear boundaries were set, my dad wasn't austere or harsh, but patient and loving. Once I was given a book as a Sunday School attendance award which I was too young to read properly for myself, so Dad would sit me on his knee, week by week, and read me the enthralling Ugandan missionary adventure of Alexander MacKay, *'The Wizard of the Great Lake'*. And to this day indelible in my mind, is the moment in the hallway of our house, when he walked past me, patting me softly on the head and telling some invisible third party in the room, *"This boy will go into the ministry one day."*

So how did I get from *there* to *there*?

I don't know how. I just know I did. *There* to *there* is what happens with prodigals. Even 2,000 years ago, Jesus wasn't making up some new narrative. His parables were real life observations that everyone, from broken-hearted fathers to desperately lost souls, could instantly identify with, discover daylight in, draw hope from. Through the Prodigal Son story, Jesus was speaking of the history and present wanderings of His own countrymen. He was comforting the hopeful and pointing them to a good posture as they awaited the much longed for wanderers' return. He was reviving hope in distraught mums and dads. Who knows, there may even have been a storm-tossed prodigal within earshot as he told the story? There might even be a prodigal reading this right now?

The prodigal writing this finally came to the end of himself on the overnight of Friday 5th and Saturday 6th February 1982. I'd been out with an increasingly concerned and gradually distancing group of friends, drinking an awful lot of alcohol since early on the Friday. One of the marks of losing our senses is the extent to which we deceive ourselves and others with our thoughts and words, while knowing in our hearts exactly what we intend to do. So, early afternoon on the Friday, I went out for a 'couple of drinks' – this is how obsessive-compulsive people often pretend!

By the time it got to 2am on the Saturday, the parties were over, everyone was gone, and I found myself wandering around, locked outside in the cold, and hungry. Having lost my keys and unable to remember where I'd been, I had no idea where to begin to look. But first things first, I needed to eat.

I made my way round to the refectory block, slid open a tall, narrow window, and wriggled sideways through the meagre gap. Inside, I prised open vertical serving area shutters, contorted my body through kitchenware storage, crept round aluminium surfaces to an industrial sized refrigerator, and pulled out a block of cheese, a loaf of bread and large apple pie.

Back outside again, I still had the problem, keyless, of how to get into my building. Pretty much everyone was in bed, with just one top floor light on. Taking a handful of small pebbles from the ground, I flung them upwards and, moments later, the window opened. It was Paul, a second-year medic who'd been in some of the same places as I over the previous twelve hours.

"Matty! What you doing?"

I told him I'd lost my keys, so he threw his out the window. With no key for my own room, I made my way upstairs.

There appeared to be a small, cosy, after-party going on in his room and, not one to arrive empty-handed, I proceeded to pull out from under my jumper a sizable multi-pack of cheese, loaf of bread and catering-sized apple pie.

"Anyone hungry?"

They were not hungry.

But they were probably embarrassed and certainly uncomfortable. One by one, as people will do when a drunk person crashes in on their conversation, they gave their excuses and made their exits for the night.

Paul was left with me.

I don't know how our conversation got there, but deep into the night it turned to God. My final contribution was to mention *Ma Satya Bharti*, a book by Bhagwan Shree Rajneesh on the topic of love.

At that point, Paul said, *"Listen to what the Bible says about love ..."*

I had little idea but, like myself, Paul, whose friend had supplied me with cannabis at another party only weeks earlier, was another prodigal.

Reaching up to his shelf, Paul, to my surprise, pulled down a Bible and began to read ...

"If I speak with the tongues of men and of angels, but do not have love, I have become a noisy gong or a clanging cymbal. If I have the gift of prophecy, and know all mysteries and all knowledge; and if I have all faith, so as to remove mountains, but do not have love, I am nothing. And if I give all my possessions to feed the poor, and if I surrender my body to be burned, but do not have love, it profits me nothing ..."

As Paul read, I was back at that place again, the place I'd been in my parents' bedroom a year ago. I'd got the help I needed from God that night, then walked away from Him. But amazingly, God hadn't walked away from me. His offer was still there. God was giving me a second chance ...

"... Love is patient, love is kind and is not jealous; love does not brag and is not arrogant, does not act unbecomingly; it does not seek its own, is not provoked, does not take into account a wrong suffered, does not rejoice in unrighteousness, but rejoices with the truth; bears all things, believes all things, hopes all things, endures all things ..."

I may have been physically drunk, but spiritually I was coming to my senses. At 4 o'clock in the morning, with everyone gone to bed, I was waking up. Within me, I knew that if I didn't say yes there and then, I never would. I realised it was now or never. As I came to my right mind, tears began to well up in my eyes and my dam of resistance finally began to give way ...

"Love never fails; but if there are gifts of prophecy, they will be done away; if there are tongues, they will cease; if there is knowledge, it will be done away. For we know in part and we prophesy in part; but when the perfect comes, the partial will be done away. When I was a child, I used to speak like a child, think like a child, reason like a child; when I became a man, I did away with childish things. For now we see in a mirror dimly, but then face to face ..."

As Paul was reading, the thing that really broke me was that God was still speaking to me.

I had entered Paul's room that night at the end of myself. My overdraft limit was reached only 4 weeks into a new term. My studies were non-existent, and I was on the verge of dropping out. My friends were withdrawing because it wasn't funny anymore. My weekends had merged into each other in one continuous binge. I was a chain-smoking, nail-biting, hand-tremoring nervous wreck who'd walked away from what I knew to be good and right. What's more, I fully understood that in doing all of that, I was personally saying a wilful, stubborn *"No!"* to God.

And here He was, still speaking to me as decent people were making polite apologies and leaving the room.

I didn't know any prayers but, like the Prodigal, no one needed to tell me what to say to my Father. With tears now pouring down my face, broken, I began to plead, *"Forgive me, Jesus. Forgive me, Jesus. Forgive me, Jesus …"*

Paul looked up from his Bible. *"What's happening, Matty?"*

The same Holy Spirit who was breaking me in pieces soon showed him what was happening, and something began to take a grip of him now too. His eyes welled up.

While all this was going on, something else was increasingly distracting me. I'd probably gone at least an hour or more without a cigarette. As Paul looked at me, asking what was happening, I found myself, by force of habit, turning to open my tin of tobacco to hand-roll a cigarette (which was all this student could afford).

But I was coming to my senses. I realised how ridiculous this was. Here was God the Saviour, entering conversation with me and offering me forgiveness. And here was I replying, 'Hold on a minute,

Lord, I'm just going to have a smoke and I'll be back to accept in a minute!'

Yes, right!

Like, after all His patience, after all I've personally done to Him, I'm seriously going to have *Him* waiting around for *me*, doing things on *my* terms, *Him* fitting in with *my* habits, accommodating *my* convenience.

When the Prodigal Son came to his senses, he knew exactly the actions he needed to take, where he needed to go, what he needed to say and do. And then he followed through. This is what repentance is, and it's the evidence that sinners have truly come to their senses.

In that moment, I knew the very first thing I needed to do, if I was to come home to the Father.

I told Paul what was going on inside me and that now I had a choice: either return to the way I was before and carry on with life my terms, or pick up my tin of Golden Virginia, representative of the whole lifestyle I'd rejected Him for, walk across the room, throw it in the bin, then get down on my knees and surrender my life to God, on God's terms.

Paul watched me do it, and I was born again that night. The other prodigal in the room returned to his Father that night too, and we began to meet daily to read the Bible and pray.

Paul gave me the Bible he read from as a gift. Appropriately, he scribbled on the inside cover, *"Matty, I love you in Jesus. I Corinthians 13."*

Final Thoughts

There were ten or fifteen Christians living in Wolfson Hall the night I came to my senses, but none of them had any idea what God was doing with these two prodigals, under their own roof, while they slept. This gives me great hope for our land today, despite the limitations and shortcomings of our churches, where it's so easy to become isolated and insulated from the depths to which many have sunk.

Yet the One whom Tim Keller describes as the 'prodigal God' (because of His 'reckless grace') will never close the door, even to those who have walked away from an astonishing spiritual heritage. No matter how far we wander or how low we sink, God still runs out to meet us, embraces us, speaks to us, welcomes us home, and rejoices over us.

He is the God who is still waiting, no matter how long it takes until we finally come to our senses.

He is the God who stays in the room as decent people distance themselves, make polite excuses, and sensibly leave.

For you, for any person, for any people whose senses have dimmed, the heart of God has never changed.

And His call remains: *Come home!*

Printed in Great Britain
by Amazon

18406224R00031